$19.95

D1221336

11/06

SOCRATES

Mason Crest Publishers, Inc.
370 Reed Road
Broomall, Pennsylvania 19008
866-MCP-BOOK (toll free)

Illustrations copyright © 1999 Iassen Ghiuselev
Published in association with
Grimm Press Ltd., Taiwan

1 3 5 7 9 8 6 4 2

Library of Congress Cataloging-in-Publication Data:

on file at the Library of Congress.

ISBN 1-59084-150-6
ISBN 1-59084-133-6 (series)

Great Names

SOCRATES

Mason Crest Publishers

Philadelphia

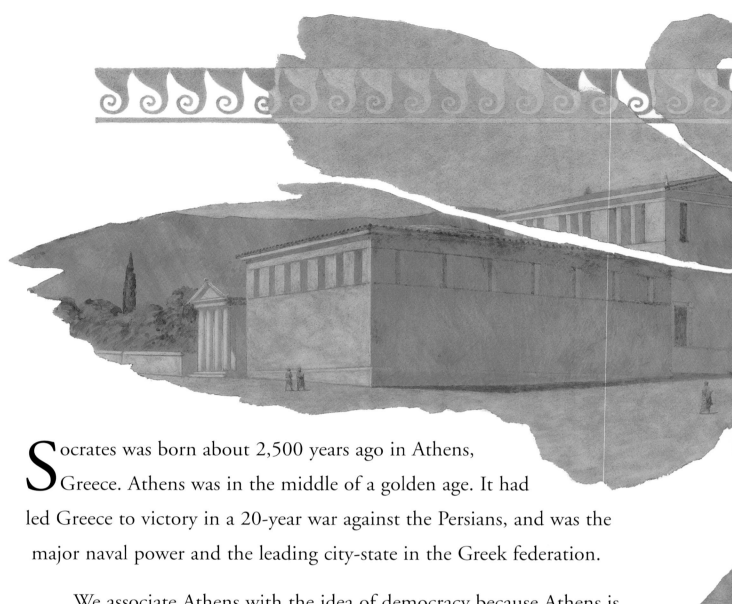

Socrates was born about 2,500 years ago in Athens, Greece. Athens was in the middle of a golden age. It had led Greece to victory in a 20-year war against the Persians, and was the major naval power and the leading city-state in the Greek federation.

We associate Athens with the idea of democracy because Athens is where the democratic form of government was born. It was a highly cultured city, where literature, art, science, and philosophy flourished. But out of a population of 400,000 people, 250,000 were slaves.

Athens's ancient form of democracy extended only to the city-state's citizens, who owned property and could vote. The majority slave population, which cleaned the houses, cared for the children, and farmed the land, was not included. As a result, there was little for the citizens to do. They had time

to amuse themselves. Perhaps this is why so many new ideas appeared around this time.

As the saying goes, what goes up must come down. Greece was no exception. The relationship between the member states of the federation eventually soured. Athens, having control of the Aegean Sea, dictated to the other states, and did more or less as it pleased. On several occasions, when conflicts of interest arose, it even attacked its fellow states.

The day came when the other states decided they had had enough. They decided to fight back. With the support and protection of the powerful Spartan army, they launched a war against Athens that lasted 27 years.

Both sides had victories and defeats in the war, but it was not until Athens lost most of its navy in a devastating ambush that the other states began to get the upper hand. Nevertheless, Athens continued to fight on stubbornly for another nine years, despite gradually getting weaker and weaker. After its allies deserted it one by one, its economy collapsed. Hungry and tired, the people lost the will to fight. Eventually Athens was forced to admit defeat.

Socrates lived through Athen's decline and fought in the war, apparently rather bravely. He often puzzled over the collapse of such a great civilized city-state. How had it happened? Was it solely because the people were hungry and defeated? He thought that perhaps the real reasons were that Athens had grown proud and self-important, and its people cared too much for material pleasures and neglected the spiritual side of life. As he put it: "Athens is like a fleet-footed horse grown fat and lazy. I am a cattle-fly on a mission from God to wake it up. But when I bite it, not only does it not thank me, it actually tries to swat me, and then goes back to sleep."

In those days, an individual's fate was closely tied to the fate of the state. If the state was defeated, its people were taken as slaves.

Athens won many wars and as a result acquired many slaves. History records one of its representatives as saying, "There's no point in complaining. It is the custom that when you lose a war you must give up your women and children to be slaves. Everyone knows and accepts this."

Socrates was a stocky man and had great stamina. Even in winter he would go out to fight in bare feet. He did not have a pretty face either; in fact he was rather ugly. He has been described as having protruding eyes, a flat nose, and thick lips, and he was so squat and short that he looked like a wine barrel when seated and a duck when walking. But his intelligence impressed everyone.

His father is thought to have been a stone mason; his mother a mid-wife. He later claimed, "My work is to assist in the birth of wisdom.

Wisdom comes from the soul. I cannot give you wisdom. I can only give you knowledge." From a very young age, he was aware of a voice inside him that said "no!" whenever he thought of something bad. His voice was what we call our conscience.

There were two main schools of philo-sophical thought in Athens during Socrates' time. One was concerned with natural phenomena, the other with human behavior. Although Socrates studied the first carefully, he was more

interested in human behavior. People who belonged to the second school of thought were called the Sophists. They believed that everybody sees the world in his or her own individual way, and as these ways are different, there can be no universal truth and no reliable knowledge. Socrates thought this idea was dangerous and he set out to challenge it.

Socrates is sometimes called the "Western Confucius." Both Confucius and he were excellent teachers who inspired many generations that followed. Socrates (469 – 399 B.C.) was born ten years after Confucius (551 – 479 B.C.) died.

Socrates was more concerned with people than nature, as reflected in his statement, "My friends are not the trees outside the city, but the people living in it." Socrates' mission was the pursuit of truth. He believed that life was worthless unless one thought about it and questioned things.

The English philosopher John Stuart Mill summed up this idea when he said, "Would you rather be a suffering Socrates or a happy pig?" The pig refers to the idea of a creature that is content with its material comforts and has no desire for an intellectual life. But, actually, no one knows whether pigs are really happy or whether Socrates was really suffering.

In his youth Socrates served in the army as a soldier. As only citizens could belong to the army, and soldiers had to provide their own armor, helmet, shield, spear, and other equipment, which was rather expensive, it seems likely he was a citizen from a reasonably well-off family.

In middle age, he wandered the streets of Athens at leisure, striking up conversations with the people he met. He was a teacher, but he did not like classes or lectures because he felt one could not communicate properly there. He felt ideas could be exchanged more effectively in conversation.

He would open the conversation by stating his views on a particular subject, and then follow up by asking his listeners for their opinions. For example, he might have asked why most people blindly accept the ideas and concepts that their parents and teachers pass on to them without asking whether the ideas are valid; and how it is impossible to develop real wisdom unless one questions things.

After talking with him, many people felt confused and uncertain. Some even felt angry. Most had thought they were reasonably knowledgeable, but Socrates told them they were ignorant. One of his students said to him, "You are like an electric eel swimming around and stunning everything you touch. Everyone you talk to ends up feeling numb!" Socrates' reply was, "If it was my purpose to numb people, that would be wrong. The truth is, I, too, am ignorant and numb."

Socrates' student, Plato, compiled Socrates' conversations into the book *Dialogues*. It became a textbook of Western philosophy. Plato also became one of the world's greatest philosophers.

Socrates believed that you can only find true knowledge if you believe you know nothing. That was what he meant by ignorance, and his task was to show people that everyone was ignorant.

Socrates was not very practical, and he and his wife did not get on well. The family's main sources of income were a government pension and some inherited land, but that barely met their needs; and yet Socrates never worked for a living. Instead, he left the house early each morning and spent the day walking the streets talking to people. Moreover, although he was a teacher and had several students, he refused to accept any payment. This drove his wife to distraction.

One day, Socrates returned home happy after another day of talking to people. His wife angrily attacked him with her words. "All you do is wander the streets all day. You have never earned a penny! Our cupboards are bare. What are we supposed to eat?"

Socrates tried to ignore her, but she made such a fuss that he decided to flee the house. Little did he know she had placed a large jug of water above the door. Of course, it fell on him as soon as he opened the door; he was soaked to the skin. Socrates was not angry, however. In fact, he joked, "I should have known. It always rains after thunder," and then continued on his way.

This well-known tale earned Socrates' wife a reputation as a nag, and perhaps even lead to the saying, "If you marry a good woman, your life will be full of joy. If you marry a nag, at least you can become a philosopher."

Socrates was an easygoing sort. Once, an early-morning knock on the door awoke him. Rubbing his eyes, he went to see who was there, only to discover a stranger who said, "I'm going to a lecture by the famous Pythagoras. Do you want to come with me?" Socrates immediately got up, dressed, and went with him.

In Socrates' daily discussions, he examined and reflected on life. He felt that life was not worth living if you simply did as everyone else did and blindly accepted the values society told you to accept. He wanted everyone to

examine things for themselves, to ask why things were the way they were, and to decide for themselves what was good or bad, true or false.

Unfortunately, Socrates' habit of questioning everything was soon to get him into trouble. It started when one of his students, having nothing better to do, went to the temple and asked the gods if there was anyone more intelligent than Socrates in Athens. The answer he got was no, and he rushed to tell Socrates. But Socrates was not impressed. "I don't believe it!" he replied. "We must go in search of a man more intelligent than me so we can prove the gods are mistaken." He could not know that this would lead to his death.

I'm not a wise person. I just love wisdom. —Socrates

Philosophy is a Latin word that comes from the words *philos*, to love, and *sophia*, knowledge.

I'm not a citizen of Athens or a citizen of Greece. I am a citizen of the world. —Socrates

Socrates sought universal truths. He was not limited by place or time.

The first people Socrates went to visit were politicians. As politicians provide leadership to the people and make important decisions, he felt they ought to appreciate the concepts of morality and virtue. After discussion with them, he realized that they did not really understand what the role of the city-state was and had not thought about the real purpose of life for the thousands of people who lived in Athens. They saw their jobs as making sure no one went hungry. They did not concern themselves with educating the people or providing them with more opportunities. to use their talents and enjoy their lives.

The politicians were interested mostly in their reelection, profiting from their business contacts, fighting their neighboring states, and capturing more slaves. Socrates was disappointed in them, but it did not affect his determination to search Athens for a person more intelligent than himself.

You can tell what kind of man Socrates was from the way he acted. First of all, he was rational and independent. Rational means that he thought logically and asked questions. Philosophers are very good at being rational. They like to examine things from all angles, not just from the outside. Independent means to think for one's self about things before accepting them. Secondly, Socrates behaved with conviction and dignity. He did not worry about what other people thought of him, and he never compromised. Nor was he afraid of death. He lived courageously, believing that his soul would continue to exist in another realm after his death.

Next he went to visit the famous poets of the time, who were like the bestselling authors of today. Many people knew and loved their work, and Socrates felt they must be very wise and philosophical to be able to write so well and so movingly. But it turned out they could not really explain their own work and sometimes, especially if it was written when they had been drinking, did not even understand it.

He visited the artisans and engineers of the city, people who produced big things and small, ranging from dishes to naval ships. Surely anyone who could create such delicate and intricate objects must be intelligent, he thought. But the fact was they used blueprints made by their ancestors and had no idea why things were done the way they were.

He traveled throughout the city and visited all the people of note and importance without discovering anyone really intelligent. "Now I understand why the gods

said there was no one more intelligent than me. At least I know I know nothing, which is one thing more than the others know!" Unfortunately, during his search, Socrates managed to offend many powerful people.

The Greeks maintained that culture developed from leisure,

and that if people did not have the time to think and create,

there would be no philosophy, literature, art, or science.

When Socrates was nearly 70, he received a summons to go to court. He had been accused of two crimes: believing in gods other than the gods of Athens and corrupting young people. Socrates decided to defend himself, and as soon as the sun rose the next day, he went and stood at the door of the court. It seems he could not wait to take the witness stand and declare his innocence. While he was standing there, a young theology student approached him and asked, "Socrates, what are you doing here so early? Have you come to accuse somebody?"

"No, it's me that's being accused. I've come to defend myself," Socrates replied. "And you?" "I've come to accuse my father of disrespect to the gods," replied the young man.

"Really? What a coincidence! That's what I'm accused of. Please explain respect to me so I can explain it to the judge."

The young man told Socrates about how his family's overseer had beaten a man, and how his father then had the overseer bound and left in a gully—before sending someone to the temple to ask the gods how the overseer should be punished. The problem was that the overseer died of cold before his father received the answer.

"My father caused the overseer's death before the gods had decided what should be done with him. That is disrespect," explained the young man.

"And what is respect?" asked Socrates. "Doing what the gods approve of is respect. Doing what the gods do not approve of is disrespect," the young man answered.

"But there are so many gods. How do you know if they all think the same? Which god must approve something before it is right?" Socrates and the young man discussed this for a long time, with Socrates encouraging the young man to do what he thought was right, not what the gods approved.

At that time, the citizens of Athens took turns serving as judges in the court. There were 501 judges for Socrates' trial, most of them younger than him.

Standing on the witness stand, he said to them, "If I wanted your sympathy I could bring my wife and children with me and beg and plead with you to let me go, but I am not willing to do this because it is not what the gods want. If they did not want me to come and face my accusers today, then my voice would have told me this was wrong, but it did not, so I came.

"What is it I do everyday? I teach people philosophy. I ask them, 'Friend, don't you feel ashamed to be so disinterested in wisdom and truth, so unconcerned about your soul?'"

To the judges it seemed as though he was accusing them. Two hundred eighty-one decided he was guilty against 220 who decided he was innocent.

The law allowed anyone found guilty to suggest an alternative punishment to death, for example, exile, but Socrates was not interested. Instead he joked, "If you put me in the Pantheon and look after me well in my old age, I might be convinced to stop walking the streets looking for people to talk with." This speech further angered the judges and several of them changed their judgment to guilty.

> *Today you may judge me but tomorrow history will judge you.*
> —Socrates

Socrates was found guilty of not believing in the gods of Athens. He did believe in God actually, but not in those gods.

Socrates was an ordinary man in many ways, yet he had the strength to do what he believed and the ability to convince others through argument. He never wavered from his ideals, even in the face of death.

He searched for truth and challenged conventional wisdom, but he did not reject everything; for example, his views on God. were firm. He said, "I don't believe in Mount Olympus and all the gods supposed to live there, but I don't doubt that there is a powerful God in this universe."

He obeyed the law even though it was not perfect. When he was found guilty and put in jail, his students wanted to bribe the guards to let him escape, but he would not permit it. He said, "How can I escape? If I am innocent, history will bring me justice. If I escape, I will be a common criminal. The law may not be perfect, but it guides the way I live. I don't want to destroy the law. I want to improve it."

Socrates' discussions were about human existence. They rarely came to a conclusion, but they made people think. The question-and-answer approach he used in these discussions is common today.

When his students heard the news that Socrates had been sentenced to death, they rushed to the prison to be with him. Many cried, but Socrates quickly hushed them. He disliked tears.

Socrates accepted his fate calmly, and unlike most people, he was not afraid of his approaching death. While in prison he discussed death with his students. "After death, one of two things may happen," he said. "Either you lose all consciousness, like going to sleep but more pleasant because dreamless—or your soul will live on in another realm. If the second thing is the case, I will be able to spend my days with the saints and the sages. I may well be even happier than I am here with you."

When the time came, a guard brought him a cup of hemlock. Socrates drank it and soon began to lose the feeling in his feet. As the numbness spread up his body, he said to his followers, "I owe the God of Medicine a chicken. Please offer it on my behalf."

It was the custom of the time to make an offering to the God of Medicine if you were sick. Socrates thought that dying was like recovering from and illness. He believed "the end of life is to be like God, and the soul following God will be like him," and that death freed his spirit. He wanted to thank the gods for this.

In *Dialogues* the prison guard is quoted as saying, "I've never had a prisoner like Socrates, so gentle and polite. Most of the prisoners that are brought here are angry and complaining of great injustices, whereas Socrates acts almost as though he were back at home." The guard cried when he brought Socrates the hemlock.

Although Socrates' life was cut short, his ideas, his methods, and his example live on. Plato said, "Of all the people I knew, he was the kindest, the most intelligent and the most upright. My greatest good fortune was to be born during his lifetime."

BIOGRAPHY

Author Richard A. Bowen resides in Wisconsin with his wife Karen. He is the editor of *Spiritual Awakenings* quarterly and co-owner of Ariadne Publishers.